Twelve Days of
STORY TIME

with Lula's Collections of Children's Stories

LULA HUGHES

PAGE PUBLISHING
Conneaut Lake, PA

First originally published by Page Publishing 2022

ISBN 978-1-6624-2980-4 (pbk)
ISBN 978-1-6624-2981-1 (digital)

Contents

Acknowledgements

First, I would like to give thanks to the Lord Jesus Christ, who granted me the creative mindset to allow children to learn and dream. He has allowed me to experience obstacles throughout this writing journey, that I would not have been able to endure without his unconditional love.

Second, my loving mother, Helen, who never doubted, for a moment, my dream of becoming a children's book author would come true. She always felt optimistic and encouraged me to reach toward my goals and accomplishments. Thank you, Mother.

My completion of this book could not have been accomplished without the support of my late husband, Richard, and my children. You all provided inspiration, as well as encouragement and support when needed, and it was very much appreciated and noted. I love you all.

Finally, to my caring and supportive relatives and friends who also wished me much success. I thank you.

The Dancing Ladybug

Most mothers love flowers, but Alice's mother adored them. During the spring months, she planted in prepared soil. When summer arrived, the elegant assortment of flowers would set off her front yard. Alice and her classmate Terri enjoyed the colorful sweet-scented blossoms. When they played the hide-and-seek game, one of their hiding areas was among the flowers.

One day, Alice played the game with her three-year-old brother, Joey. She had hidden near a wide leaf plant. A two-inch reddish-spotted beetle clinging under a leaf caught her attention. She removed it from the leaf and held it in the palm of her left hand.

"Joey!" Alice shouted. "Look what I have found!"

"It's a big bug," said Joey.

"Of course. It's a ladybug," Alice told him.

"A ladybug? Let's find a man bug," replied Joey.

"You're so silly," giggled Alice. "There aren't any."

In the house, Alice told her mother, holding up her hand with the ladybug still in her palm.

"I found a ladybug, Mom!" Alice shouted excitedly.

"It's a big beautiful bug," her mom replied. "I haven't seen many that size."

Everyday Alice sat and played with the ladybug. She placed the beetle on her left hand fingertips. She enjoyed the ticklish feeling when it crawled toward her wrist.

One day she decided to sing a song to the ladybug.

"La-la-la-la-a-a. "You're a cute little ladybug, la-la-la-la-a-a." The bug stood on its tiny hind legs and bounced its body from side to side. "This is unreal! It dances," squealed Alice. She rushed into the house shouting. "Look! Mother! I sang, and the ladybug started to dance". Alice did a little dance to demonstrate to her mother what the ladybug had done.

Shocked, Alice's mother replied, "Oh my goodness. That's fantastic! You've found a dancing ladybug."

"A dancing ladybug?" asked Joey. "Let's find a dancing man bug."

The next day, Alice told her classmate Terri all about the dancing spotted beetle.

"That's nonsense. You must be kidding," said Terri.

"If you walk home with me after school, I'll show you," replied Alice.

After the girls arrived, they went directly to the flowers.

"This wide green leaf plant is its home, and this is its favorite leaf," Alice said as she began her search for the beetle. She carefully searched the plant and looked under each leaf. She couldn't find the ladybug. It was gone. "It's around here somewhere," Alice said, trying not to worry.

Terri just folded her arms and stood waiting.

"Come help me search," yelled Alice.

"Help you search for something that doesn't exist? You're insane!" snapped Terri. "There was never a dancing ladybug, and you were just pretending."

"It does exist, and I am not insane," Alice sobbed.

"I'm going to tell the whole class about your stupid dancing ladybug story." Terri scoffed.

Alice ran into the house.

"Mother, Mother," she cried. "I can't find my dancing ladybug. It has disappeared, and I'll never see it again."

"Darling, don't panic. It's all right. I'll help you locate the talented beetle," her mother said calmly.

After a short search her mother said, "There it is! It crawled over to the next plant."

Alice sighed with relief, "Thanks, Mother." She walked toward her classmate Terri. "I found it! I found it!"

"I must see this to believe it," said Terri.

Alice sang her song, "La-la-la-a-a. You're a cute little ladybug, la-la-la-la-a-a."

Again, the dancing beetle stood on its hind legs, and bounced its little body from side to side.

"Now what do you have to say for yourself?" Alice asked Terri with her hands on her hips.

"Unbelievable, but true! I am sorry. I doubted you and threatened to tell our classmates," Terri replied.

"I am too," said Alice. "But I'm glad that you apologized, and we are still best friends."

"Now is it okay if I tell the class about your dancing ladybug?" asked Terri.

"Certainly." answered Alice. "You can also tell the class that I'll never let it get away again."

A Tree Full of Birds

One warm spring morning, Dawn and her brother Roger got up before the sun rose to wait for their friends, Ruby and Paul, who are also sister and brother. The friends lived about a mile away from one another but could take a shortcut through the woods when they go camping near the lake.

After Ruby and Paul arrived, the girls packed popcorn, cookies, and strawberry punch while the boys got the fishing poles. They gathered their things and walked to the camping area. At the campsite, their tent sat near a beautiful dwarf plum tree. The single stem was four feet tall. The head of the branches and leaves reached out in an upward position, shaping the tree in a circle. It had small green leaves and white blossoms on every branch. The blossoms left a spring fresh scent that filled the air.

"Come quick, you guys," said Roger as he led the way down the narrow path.

"What is it?" Paul asked.

"Look. In the prettiest tree in the woods, two birds are sharing a worm," said Roger. "They are pulling from each end trying to tear it apart."

"Birds!" shouted Dawn as more birds fly toward the tree. "It would make a tree full of birds if they all land on it."

"Birds are too active to land on one tree," said Paul, "unless something is there to attract them."

"The sweet smell of white blossoms and the warm sunshine just aren't enough," said Ruby.

"One worm couldn't feed them all," said Roger. "I'll throw them some popcorn."

"Come on, let's go fishing," said Roger.

"I'll be the first to catch a fish," said Paul.

"No, you won't," said Roger. "I'll be the first."

The boys grabbed their fishing poles and ran to the lake.

"Do you want to play, school, in the tent," asked Dawn. "I brought my book titled *All About Birds*."

"No," said Ruby. "I don't want to read that book. Some of the words are hard for me to pronounce."

"I'll let you pretend to be the teacher," insisted Dawn.

"You think you know it all because you can read a book from the sixth grade!" snapped Ruby.

"You're jealous," said Dawn.

"I don't want to play *school*!" said Ruby, running to the lake.

"What's wrong?" asked Paul.

"I don't want to play *school* with *miss-know-it-all*," said Ruby.

"Is there a reason for you to get so upset?" asked Paul.

"Maybe not," said Ruby. "I do owe her an apology."

Dawn walked through the woods alone. By the time she came to the lake, a big black dog was running after her. She screamed and cried as the dog chased her up the hill and around the lake. Roger and Paul pulled their fishing poles from the lake while Ruby clapped her hands to get the dog's attention. Roger yelled for the dog to stop, but he did not stop and continued to chase after Dawn.

"The tent! The tent!" Roger yelled for Dawn to go back to the camping area and get inside the tent, but Dawn ran towards the lake instead.

Roger yelled, "No! Stay away from the water!"

Mr. Watlow, the dog's owner, heard the screams and came running up the hill. By the time he got to the top of the hill, Ruby was patting the dog on the head.

"Blackie," Mr. Watlow called, and the dog ran to his owner. "I'm sorry, kids. I let him off his leash for only a moment. He is really a friendly dog and wanted to play."

"It's all right," said Dawn. "He startled me, and when I turned around, he was running towards me."

"I'll see to it that I never take him off his leash again during our daily walks," Mr. Watlow said as he smiled and walked away with Blackie.

"Dawn, are you okay?" Ruby asked. "I'm sorry when I said you thought that you knew it all. I was being a bit jealous."

"Yes, I am fine. Thank you," replied Dawn. "I can't know it all. When I was being chased by the big black dog, I ran toward the water instead of running toward the tent."

"You were afraid," said Ruby. "I'm just glad that you are okay and you're still my best friend."

Back at the camping site, there was an array of beautiful colors. As the kids approached, they noticed blue, black, orange, red, yellow, and brown birds eating the popcorn from the ground.

"I have an idea," said Dawn. "The popcorn is a way to attract the birds."

"That's a wonderful idea," said Paul. "You are a smart kid."

They cut pieces of fishing lines into sixteen inches, then they poked a hole in each kernel of popcorn with a fishing hook, and they threaded them. Paul and Roger climbed the tree while Dawn and Ruby handed them the threaded popcorn.

"Let's stand away from the tree," said Roger, "to watch for a tree full of birds."

Within seconds, more birds began to appear. And then even more birds began to appear.

"There are so many birds in the tree that it seems as if it's decorated with colorful lights," said Ruby.

"Next time let's bring a camera so we can capture this moment of a tree full of birds, forever," said Dawn.

The Grape House

The Jenson family live in a small town called Appleland. Their home is in the shape of an apple with the chimney in the shape of an apple stem. The family has grown over the years and their house is becoming too small for their needs.

Mrs. Jenson complained for the third time. "This house is too small. We must find a larger one."

"My room is very small. My dollhouse will not fit in it," said Sally. "I'd rather have a bigger one."

"I like to play football," said Todd. "And I rather have a bigger front yard."

"All right, all right, we'll find a larger house with a big front yard," agreed Mr. Jenson.

They all went to search for the house of their dreams.

"Look," said Sally pointing her finger as they rode along. "Those houses are for sale."

"They are beautiful," said her father. "But your mother prefers a more appealing house."

Her mother agreed. "Yes. Charming, unique, and appealing. All-in-one."

"A quarter of a mile further is my friend Doug's fruit store. I'll stop there for a short visit," suggested Mr. Jenson.

"I would like that," said Todd. "I'm getting hungry."

After they arrived, Mr. Jenson went inside.

"Hello, Doug," he said. "It's been a long time since I've seen you."

"Yes, it has been quite a while," replied Mr. Jenson.

"What brings you to the Grapeland area?"

"We're searching for a bigger and better home". Maybe in this area we'll find the house of our dreams."

"There are charming homes in Grapeland. I really hope you find the one that fits your family's needs," said Doug.

"If it's the right house, it will fit our needs," said Mr. Jenson. "And again, we may find just what we are looking for."

"Good luck to you all, and we would love to welcome you to our Grapeland community," said Doug.

Soon the Jenson's arrived to see the houses in Grapeland.

"My goodness!" exclaimed Mrs. Jenson. "They are all spectacular. It's very hard to choose. This one is unique, appealing, and charming. The Grape house is just what I had dreamed of."

Sally said excitedly, "This is going to be my room, it is a lot bigger!"

"I get to play football with all of my friends in this big front yard," Todd told his 5-year-old sister.

"This is the kind of house we are looking for. Unusual but beautiful," said Mr. Jenson. "Let's buy it."

The Jenson family chose a grape house in Grapeland. It has grapevine trimming and grape bunch shaped windows and doors. One-third of the backyard had clusters of brilliant juicy smooth-skinned edible fruit attached to the woody flexible stems. The climbing, clinging, and twining around makes a vinery landscape for the Jenson's new home.

As Mrs. Jenson looked toward the grapy view she said, "Grapeland is a lovely town with grapes galore."

"What are we going to do with them?" asked Sally.

"I'm going to eat them," answered Todd as he picked some from a low cluster.

"I've a better idea," said Mr. Jenson. "We will sell them for a profit."

After the Jenson's purchased their home, they invited Doug over for a visit. Doug was in pure amazement at the view of their lovely grape house.

"Wow, this home is amazing!" exclaimed Doug. "I love the many grapevines surrounding the house, and you guys surely have enough room for everyone. The yard is full of crimson, black, blue, yellow, green, orange, and pink clustered grapes. The wide array of colors coming up the walkway captured my attention."

Mr. Jenson said, "Thanks so much, Doug. There were many homes to choose from here in Grapeland, but this one is our dream home. Doug, we invited you over to sample some homemade Jenson's grape jelly and jam to place on the shelves in your fruit store".

Mrs. Jenson placed a spoonful of Jenson's jelly and a spoonful of Jenson's jam in front of Doug. Sally then placed a slice of toast on the side. The family watched silently as Doug took his first bite.

"Tasty. I could eat a whole jar," replied Doug.

Mr. Jenson and Doug shook hands. Sally and Todd ran outside excitedly, and Mrs. Jenson smiled from ear to ear in their charming, unique, and appealing all-in-one Grape home. The Jenson family sold Jenson jam and jelly to not only Doug's fruit store but also local supermarkets in the Grapeland area.

The Magic Lemon

Ben Wayside's mother had a fruit tree collection in her backyard. Each time his uncle Tommy visited from his fruit orchard, he would bring a different kind of fruit tree. When Ben was several months old, he brought a lemon tree. Ben's mother always had enough space to add another tree in the yard. She is a member of a Lady's Club. Sometimes she donates fruits and refreshments after the meetings. After school, Ben usually goes bike riding with his neighbor Rhonda. After he discovered the lemons on the tree for the very first time, he went outside to play under it.

One day, he saw an oversized lemon hanging among the normal sized ones.

"Mother, come here," he called. "There's a lemon nearly the size of my big football."

She came running from the kitchen and into the backyard. "It's incredible for a lemon to grow that size," she said.

"Mother, I believe there is something magical about this tree. It's the one my uncle brought from his orchard when I was only a few months old," said Ben.

"Nonsense," his mother said. "There is no such thing as magic fruit or tree."

Rhonda rode in on her bike. "Are you going bike riding today?" she asked.

"Wow!" said Rhonda. "I have never seen such a big lemon. Well, I have to go for my bike ride, I'll see you later."

"My next club meeting is tomorrow. I would like to donate lemonade after the meeting. Would you please pick some lemons?" his mother asked.

"I'd be happy too," said Ben.

As he began to pick the lemons, a voice said, *Do not Pick lemons from this tree*! Ben stopped and turned his head toward the voice which sounded as if it came from a tunnel. When he didn't hear the voice, again he continued to pick more lemons. Again, the voice spoke, *DO NOT PICK ANY MORE LEMONS FROM THIS TREE!* in a louder voice.

Ben stopped, "I heard a voice, but I don't see anyone. It must be Rhonda pretending to be invisible."

At that moment, Rhonda arrived.

"Hi, I'm back from my bike ride," she said.

"Where have you been?" asked Ben.

"I went bike riding, remember?" Rhonda replied.

"Yes, but—were you hiding near the lemon tree pretending to be invisible?" he asked.

"No, Ben. It wasn't me," answered Rhonda.

"Would you like to help me pick lemons for my mother?" asked Ben.

"I would love too, but I must be getting home soon. I promise to help when I return," said Rhonda.

Ben became curious. *If it wasn't Rhonda's voice, not his voice, and of course, it was not his mother's voice, then whose voice could it be?* wondered Ben as he continued to pick the lemons.

Do not touch another lemon, said the voice.

"Who are you?" asked Ben.

I'm the magic lemon, answered the voice.

"A magic lemon!" squealed Ben. "Oh! I knew there was something magical about this tree. But where are you? I can hear you, but I can't see you."

I am invisible, replied the voice. *You can't see me.*

"Why can't I pick lemons from my very own tree in my very own backyard?" Ben asked.

I control the lemons on this tree, said the magic lemon.

"I don't understand," said Ben. "My uncle brought this tree to me from his fruit orchard seven years ago. How did you get to be a part of it?" ask Ben.

I've been at the root of this tree for seven years. It's my home. When it grew, I grew, said the magic lemon.

"Show your face you magic lemon! I'm sick of talking to a voice anyway!" Ben said angrily.

The oversized yellow egg-shaped fruit jumped down to the ground. Its eyes, mouth, arms, legs, and feet all appeared right in front of Ben's eyes.

"There you are. A magic lemon! You really do exist, my very own magic lemon!" yelled Ben. "You will be my secret magic lemon friend," he said.

"No one else is allowed to pick lemons from this tree but you since we grew with the tree together," said the magic lemon. "And I want to show you a bit of magic."

Suddenly all the lemons disappeared and so did the magic lemon.

"No! No!" cried Ben. "Make them reappear! Magic lemon! Magic lemon please come back! My mother needs lemonade for her meeting," begged Ben.

The lemons reappeared and so did the magic lemon.

"Oh wow. You really can do magic," said Ben. "Do you think you can magically pick these lemons and make the lemonade for my mother?"

"Why of course," said the magic lemon. "But we need a secret magic word so that I will always know it's you."

Ben thought for a moment. "Magic orchard!" he screamed. "No one will ever guess that."

The magic lemon replied, "Okay. Let's hear the magic words."

Ben closed his eyes and said quietly, "Magic orchard," and when he opened them, there were just enough lemons picked for the lemonade, but before he could get excited Rhonda appeared.

"Ben, what are you doing with your eyes closed, lets pick these lemons for your mother," she said. "Wait! You're already done. I wasn't gone that long. How did you pick all those lemons?" Rhonda asked.

"Well, it's my secret. Can you help get them in the house?" replied Ben.

Ben and Rhonda took the lemons to the kitchen and prepared the fruit for freshly squeezed homemade lemonade.

Ben's mom kissed him on the head and said, "Thanks so much for making the lemonade. I saw the pitcher full in the refrigerator. I'm not sure how you had so much time to pick lemons and make the lemonade but thank you." "How did you do it?" his mom asked.

Ben smiled and said, "Well, it's my secret."

With the leftover lemons, they all made lemon meringue pie, and Ben kept his promise to the magic lemon.

Blair's Live Bird Collection

The Mason's moved into a big house which sat on a small hill. They knew between the two of them, Blair and her mother, there would be plenty of extra room. Blair and her mother were safe, and the neighbors were friendly. That's when Blair met Molly.

"Hi, I'm Molly Turner. I live down the street."

"I'm Blair Mason. My mother and I are moving into this big house."

After the girls introduced themselves, Blair asked Molly to come inside and look around in their house.

"This is a very nice house," said Molly. "But it's too big for the two of you," she added.

"I have an idea, I'd love to own some pets," said Blair.

"Some pets? What kind did you have in mind?" Molly asked.

"Well, birds have always been my favorite pets," answered Blair.

"Birds, I love birds," said Molly.

"Come on, let's tell my mother."

"Mother, meet Molly my new friend. She lives down the street," said Blair.

"Hi, Molly, it was nice to have met you," she said politely.

"Mother, after we are settled in our house, may we go to the pet store? I'd love to have some pet birds," said Blair.

"Certainly. With all the extra rooms we have here in our house, I couldn't think of one reason why you couldn't have your very own bird collection," answered her mother.

Blair and her mother went to buy birds from the local pet supply store. They bought all colors and kinds that included: a yellow songbird canary, a white cockatoo with sprouting hair on his crown, a colorful talkative parrot, and a black-and-yellow long-billed toucan.

Blair was excited. "I'll call this collection Blair's live bird collection."

Friends and relatives brought birds to add to her collection. Blair's collection had grown in a very short time with the support of her friend Molly. Blair is doing her best to take proper care of the birds. She feeds them regularly; she plays with them, talks to them, and allows them to fly freely in their big home.

"Oh, Mother, I never dreamed of having my very own live bird collection. I'm very happy we moved into this big house, and glad that I met a friend like Molly. I'll always have enough space to add another bird to my live bird collection," said Blair.

You are
Invited!

Sidney is in Charge

Samantha and Sidney Hill are sister and brother. Sidney is in charge of housekeeping the week that their parents go to visit their uncle Jeff. Sidney calls Samantha, Sam; and Samantha calls Sidney, Sid. Usually they get along well, but other times they fight with each other. Mrs. Walton, their next-door neighbor could be reached if an emergency would occur.

"Here is a letter from your friend who lives in Peoria," said Sid.

"Wendy?" asked Sam excitedly, ripping off the top of the envelope, eager to read what was inside. "It's an invitation to her birthday party, Saturday at noon," she said.

"That is when the summer music band practice begins," said Sid.

"Are you interested in the music band practice this summer?" asked Sam.

"Of course, this summer I become one of the lead guitar players," answered Sid.

"Oh, that's wonderful. Mother and Father will be very proud. One of these days I would like to go and watch you practice," Sam said.

"I would like that too," said Sid. "I also enjoy being a fan of the music band, it's a terrific group," she added. "What would Wendy like for a birthday present?" asked Sid.

"Jewelry is one of her favorites. A ring would make a lovely gift," answered Sam.

"A perfect fit jade would be very impressing," said Sid. "I have band practice on Saturday, and you must stay with the Walton's," demanded Sid.

"I am invited to Wendy's birthday party," said Sam.

"But Mother and Father are on their trip and will not return home until Tuesday. You couldn't possibly go to the party," added Sid.

"Oh no, brother dear, that's not fair. You have band practice, and Mother and Father are on their trip, and I am invited to a birthday party. Wendy will be very disappointed if I do not show. There is no reason for this!" Sam said angrily.

"If it means that much to you, I will phone Mother at Uncle Jeff's," suggested Sid.

"Hello, Mother, this is Sid."

"Hi dear, is everything all right?" asked Mother.

"Yes, we are fine. Sam is invited to Wendy's birthday party on Saturday at noon," answered Sid.

"We will not return home until Tuesday; how would she get there?" asked Mother.

"By train. I will make her reservations," answered Sid.

"So you have this all figured out?" Mother replied.

"Yes, Mother. Sam really wants to go, and I have band practice," Sid replied.

"All right, she can go but not alone, and you are in charge to make the final decision," Mother said.

Sid replied, "Okay, Mom. I will let you know what I decide. Talk with you later."

Sid took a seat on the couch to think about this situation. He had band practice, and Sam had a party to attend. She could attend the party but not make the trip alone. So that left Sid with the choice to either accompany Sam on the trip or go to band practice—and Sam would miss the birthday party. Sid spent a little more time thinking, and he finally made a decision.

Sid called Sam over, "Sam, come here. I'm on the couch."

Sam walked in with tears in her eyes.

"Are you calling to tell me I can't go to the party?" Sam said.

"Well, Mother said you can go, just not alone," Sid replied.

"You have band practice, so that means you can't go with me," Sam sobbed.

"Don't cry, sister Sam, we have some packing to do for our trip," said Sid.

"What about your Saturday noon band practice?" asked Sam, looking confused.

"I will go to band practice next Saturday," answered Sid.

"It's obvious that the trip to Wendy's means a lot to you," he said.

"You are the best brother a sister could have, to give up something that means a lot to you too," said Sam.

"I would have to agree with you, Sam. That's why Mom left Sidney in charge," said Sidney.

They both chuckled as they headed to call Mom.

FAMILY
REUNION

Mother Bunny's Missing Pie

On one of the nicest days of the summer, the bunnies thought they would all get up very early.

"It's a beautiful day to attend a family reunion," said Mother Bunny.

"Yes, it's a wonderful day. And to see all of our relatives again is always a pleasure," Father Bunny said.

"It makes me feel very happy when Aunt Bunny say, 'Oh my! You have grown,'" said Daughter Bunny.

"Playing sports and winning bike races with my cousins are very exciting," said Son Bunny.

After their nutritious breakfast, Son and Daughter Bunny went out to play.

"Let's pack a basket of goodies to take along," said Mother Bunny.

"Some carrots would be appetizing," Father Bunny said. And away he went to the garden.

Mother Bunny decided to bake some pies. "Three would be sufficient," she said. After the pies were baked, she removed two of them from the oven. "They are very hot. I'll place them on the table to cool," she said.

"In several hours, the family reunion will begin. We must get dressed now," said Mother Bunny, and she called Son and Daughter Bunny inside.

"Those pies smell delicious," said Daughter Bunny.

"And they look tasty too," Son Bunny said as they walked into the kitchen.

"I would like to help you fill the basket with goodies," Daughter Bunny said.

"Certainly," Mother Bunny replied.

"I am completely dressed," said Son Bunny and back outside he went.

"Father Bunny will be home soon to dress for the family reunion," said Mother Bunny. Mother Bunny was dressed and on her way to the kitchen.

"Are you ready to help me fill the basket?" Mother Bunny asked Daughter Bunny.

"No, I'm not dressed," said Daughter Bunny. "Where are my blue shorts?" she asked.

"I washed them. Wear the red shorts instead," replied Mother Bunny.

"I won't! I won't! I won't wear the red shorts!" said Daughter Bunny angrily.

"The family reunion starts soon. If you're still interested in going, I suggest that you get dressed right away," said Mother Bunny.

"Okay, Mother, I'll wear the red shorts." Daughter Bunny pouted.

Into the kitchen, Mother Bunny went to fill the basket. "Oh my goodness! I know my eyes are not deceiving me! I baked three pies," she said.

Mother Bunny searched and searched all through the kitchen but couldn't find the missing pie.

"Where is the missing pie?" asked Mother Bunny.

"I don't have any idea. I was getting dressed," said Daughter Bunny.

"Where is the missing pie?" asked Mother Bunny.

"I don't have any idea. I went out to play," said Son Bunny.

Father Bunny came home to dress for the family reunion.

"Where is the missing pie?" asked Mother Bunny.

"I went to get carrots from the garden, remember," said Father Bunny. "It is time for the family reunion, and we must leave now."

"The family reunion is about to begin, and there is no sign of the missing pie," said Mother Bunny.

"Let's not worry about the missing pie," said Father Bunny, and away they went to the family reunion.

"We are having fun," said Son and Daughter Bunny.

"This is joy and happiness," Mother and Father Bunny said.

After the family reunion, they all expressed their farewells, and away everyone went on their way home.

"I have an idea where the missing pie is," Mother Bunny said.

"Where?" asked Father, Daughter, and Son Bunny.

"I forgot to take it out of the oven," said Mother Bunny.

43

At the Pond

Many summers ago, Chance visited some relatives who lived in the South. They knew when he was a child that one of his favorite places was at the pond. About one-fourth of a mile from their house was the enormous circle-shaped still body of water stocked with many small fishes. It seems freshly dug, but it had been there for nearly a century.

One summer day, he spent the day at the pond but took in the beautiful scenery on his way there. As he strolled through the yellowish-greenish pines, a July summer breeze whisked across his face. He took a seat on a dilapidated tree stump, nearby an aged tree, that concealed shade a certain time of the day. Meditating, refreshing memories filled his mind. He was excited to get to the pond to throw out his fishing rod, because catching fish was always exciting to him. As he soaked up the sun, he noticed a squirrel with a fascinating tail. It was soft, light, and fluffy. The tail was so large.

It made Chance think if he had it as a pet, he would name him Fluff. He watched the lively energetic squirrel bounce from branch to branch and nibble on a few acorns. Soon Fluff was out of sight, and Chance was back on the road toward the pond.

Once he arrived, he remembered why he loved to visit the pond. As Chance set up his fishing pole, he noticed the gray rocks with small streams of water trickling down. He also saw green lily pads nearby as a family of white swans pushed their way through. He baited the fishing hook and threw the line into the water. But before he could get settled, the rod suddenly trembled. Something was nibbling at the bait. He was standing about three feet away from the fishing rod. He stumbled over and grabbed it with a jerk. He had reeled in an eighteen-inch mud catfish.

Staring at it for a few seconds, he felt proud but hesitated to touch it. It was huge; it fluttered, making a sound of light flapping wings. At the end of the fluttering, Chance freed the catfish from the hook and tossed it back into the sparkling pond. He was left with a sticky moist substance that coated his fingers and reminded him of his triumph in the fishing sport. The day was not even over, and Chance couldn't wait to return to the pond next year.

The End of the Season Baseball Game

Caleb is an attractive nine-year-old boy, who is well rounded and full in form with a beautiful close-cut hairstyle. When he smiles, he shows a wide grin and one dimple on his left cheek. He is self-assured, active and at times uncooperative. Ann is his friend, the tall short-haired girl. She is approximately the same age he is, but she is more of a leader than a follower and very much so sophisticated. Caleb and Ann reside near the recreation area. They spent plenty of time there enjoying the fun things that are entertaining. They are also interested in sports. Caleb is a baseball player on the Southside Baseball Team for boys. Ann is a baseball player for the North side team for girls.

One day at the park the North side baseball team went to practice for the end of the season baseball game. Caleb was at the park for pleasure.

HOME
AWAY
NORTH SIDE
01
SOUTH SIDE
01

"Hi, Ann," said Caleb.

"Hi, Caleb," said Ann.

"Our team will practice tomorrow for the end of the season baseball game," Caleb said.

"Look at my uniform, it's navy-blue with white numbers on the back of it," said Ann.

"My uniform is white with navy-blue numbers on it," said Caleb.

"Would your team like to play a baseball game with our team?" asked Ann.

"Of course," replied Caleb with self-assurance and confidence. "Our team will win, our team always wins," he added.

"Let's go ask my uncle Al, he is the coach for the North side Baseball Team," said Ann.

Ann introduced Caleb to her uncle. "Uncle Al this is Caleb, he plays on the Southside Baseball Team, and we would like to play a baseball game against his team," she told her uncle.

"I can arrange for the Southside team versus the North side team for the end of the season baseball game," said Uncle Al.

On the day of the game, Caleb stood on the home plate, swinging warm-up strokes as he waited for the pitcher to start throwing. Caleb's white uniform with navy-blue numbers on it looked adorable. After the action began, things were going great. Caleb made a home run, but the North side team scored high points also. As the game continued, Caleb didn't reach first base one time, so he was out.

"I'm safe!" he shouted.

"You are out!" Ann shouted back.

"You are all cheaters, and you are not my friend anymore!" he screamed back at Ann. "The Southside team won because I made a home run," he added.

"No, the North side team won because we scored the most points!" Ann shouted.

Uncle Al noticed the tension between the two and stepped in to resolve the issue. "Hey, what's going on guys?" he asked.

Caleb screamed, "I made a home run, my team won!"

"But we scored the most points, so my team won!" Ann screamed back.

"Hold on, you two. Caleb, did you give your all out on the field?" asked Uncle Al.

"Yeah, I did," mumbled Caleb.

Uncle Al turned to Ann and asked, "Did you give your all out on the field?"

"Yes, I did," mumbled Ann.

"And there you have it. As long as you try your best, your best will always be good enough. Both teams are winners in my eyes. You both should be proud of yourselves, each other, and your teams because you gave your all out on the field." Uncle Al winked his eye and walked away.

Caleb and Ann shook hands and became friends again.

"We can't win them all," Caleb said.

"Maybe the Southside team will win the next end of the season game," said Ann.

Jason's Pet Kitten

In the neighborhood where Jason Smith lives, there aren't very many children his age. Most of the time, he plays alone or with his kitten Cutie. Cutie is a very gentle and cute cat, that is how she got her name. She strayed away from her old home, and Jason welcomed her into a new one.

Inside when they play together, Cutie jumps on tabletops, living room furniture; and she also clings to the top of the drapes on the windows. When outside, she interferes with nestled birds by climbing small trees. Jason amuses himself by chasing after Cutie and throwing a ball of yarn for her to entertain herself by going after it. They became real good friends and are truly fond of each other.

Jason's cousin Tony lives about two miles away with his pet puppy named Rowie. They take turns spending weekends at each other's house. One of the weekends that Tony spent at Jason's house, he brought along his pet puppy Rowie. *It is going to be a long night*, the eight-year-old boy thought as the evening progressed. They were very eager for the next morning to arrive.

Finally, morning came and up-and-out they went to play. Then about dawn, Tony and Jason approached a nearby bench to watch their pets occupy themselves.

"Kittens and puppies don't get along very well. They love to fight," Tony said.

"It seems to be that Cutie and Rowie are getting along fine. Just look at their lively moves," Jason said.

"That's because Rowie has a bone and Cutie has a ball of yarn," Tony said.

"How did your pet puppy get the name Rowie?" Jason asked.

"My favorite stuffed animal, a goldish-brown pup was named Rowie. So when I saw a puppy the same color at the pet shop, I knew right away I would call him Rowie too," Tony stated. "How did your kitten get her name?" Tony asked.

"She is very cute, so I called her Cutie," Jason said.

"Rowie is a very talented puppy he does dog tricks," Tony told Jason. "Let me show you what he can do," he added as they jogged away from the bench. "Rowie, roll over. Sit. Go catch the ball!" Tony yelled.

"That's wonderful! He is a perfect little pet. Let me show you what Cutie can do," said Jason.

Jason picked up Cutie and sat her in front of him and Tony. He held his hand up in the form of a high five. And before he could speak, Cutie raised her paw and gently tapped his hand.

"Wow, I've never seen a cat give a high five. That's cool," said Tony.

"Hold on, there is more," said Jason. Cutie sat on her hind legs as if reaching for the treat but instead held out her paw to shake hands with Jason.

"Cutie really is talented just like Rowie," said Tony.

"I agree," said Jason. "Although they are different and like different things, they are both equally special to us."

The Stray Kitten

During the months of summer usually in the afternoon, Katie would take leisure breaks in the backyard. She would go directly to the swinging hammock, one of her favorite relaxing things to do. Her hammock hung eight feet in length and was tied at each end around the trunk of two narrow-leaf trees. From a very short distance, the narrow-leaf trees and the exquisite colorful flowers that covered the silver-wired fence, set off the V-shaped yard.

It's a lovely scenery, Katie thought as she swung backward and forward, then noticed a stray kitten that had jumped over the wire fence. She was no longer alone in the backyard.

"Hello there," Katie said to the stray kitten. She placed her hand out to the kitten, and she moved around in a lively manner.

"You are a gentle little kitten," Katie told her.

"Are you lost?" Katie asked as she started to notice her gray fur, green eyes, pink nose, and four white paws.

Unfortunately, Katie never owned a pet, and she was not familiar with how to care for them, but this one was beautiful.

"It is getting late. We must try to find your home," Katie said as she scooped the kitten into her hands. Katie went to several houses in the neighborhood; no one had ever seen or owned her. Katie returned to the backyard to put her down.

Maybe you can find your home from here, Katie thought.

She sat on the hammock and watched as the kitten lay down underneath.

Katie could not find the kitten's home and did not want her to be abandoned for the second time. She suddenly had a wonderful idea; she could give the kitten to Ty, the boy next door. He was new to the neighborhood and could surely use a new friend.

The little stray kitten was given to Ty, and he named her Sue. He is taking proper care of her, and she is a happy kitten. Katie felt good to have found Sue a new home.

Ross

Many residents live about a quarter of a mile from the outdoor recreation area. The rectangle-shaped lawn formed the playground that was full of open space for picnics, bird watching and many other activities that the community members loved. From a parked car came a boy named Ross moving at a fast pace. At the end of the steep hill was a water fountain that Ross came running too. He stopped for only one drink, but before he left, he had gotten several. After quenching his thirst, he continued to push the button to watch the stream of water, rise and fall.

He looked around the playground as if he was thinking about what to do next. It seemed as though he admired the sandbox, because he went directly to it. A light gentle breeze shivered his solid outfit as he kneeled in a leaning position. Making small mounds of sand, he cupped his hands around each mound making

sure the peaks were firm. He expected more children to be at the playground, enjoying the last summer days before winter begins.

"I will spin you on the merry-go-round," a voice of a long-haired girl said to Ross and some of the other children playing along with him.

Suddenly being the last one, Ross got up on his feet and ran with a skip to join the girl and the other children.

"Spin us faster and faster," said Ross to the girl.

"Let us take turns," said the girl to Ross.

By this time, all the other children had left, so very cooperative, he jumped from the revolving platform. After giving her one of his intense spins, he stood back to watch her spin. At the beginning, she was a bit surprised but excited. Then Ross started to spin her faster and faster and faster. Instantly the girl became frightened.

"I'm afraid, slow me down!" she yelled.

"This is fun," said Ross with a penetrating grin. He continued to aggravate her by spinning the merry-go-round as fast as he could.

"Slow me down!" she shouted. "I mean it this time! Stop!" she cried.

"Okay, okay," Ross mumbled.

Ross did not seem to mind that she had yelled at him. "I'm sorry," he said when the girl finally stopped spinning.

"It was so fun spinning you fast. I didn't stop to think how you felt or that you could get hurt."

"You are right. Merry-go-rounds can be fun, but kids can also fall off if being spun too fast. But I am sorry too for yelling."

"That's okay," said Ross. "What is your name?"

"My name is Amy," she said.

"My name is Ross. Would you like to go to the swings? I promise to not push you so fast and stop when you tell me to stop."

They left roaming through the playground happy to have met each other and starting a new friendship.

About the Author

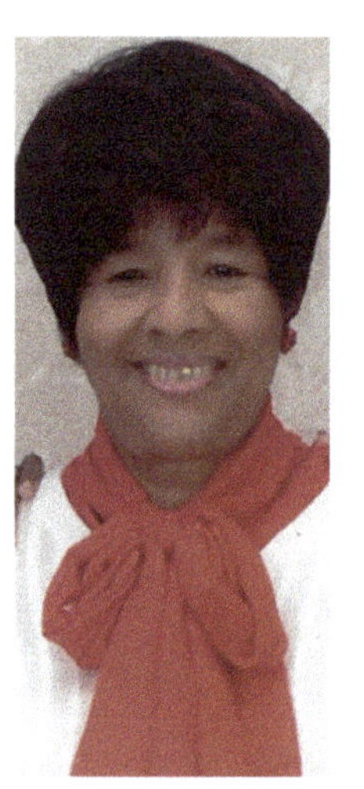 Lula Mae Hughes was born and raised in Woodville, Mississippi, surrounded by her parents and seven siblings. She later moved to St. Louis, Missouri, where she married and raised her three daughters.

Lula's love of reading came from spending long hot summers outdoors and spending time teaching her younger siblings. She was able to truly set her passion into motion when her career path led her to teaching preschool children. During this time, she was inspired to step out on faith and become a children's book author, sharing stories to children across the world while encouraging them to dream and imagine a fun, colorful world through her descriptive writing.

Today Lula has created a collection of her stories for children and adults to enjoy. She is now retired with seven grandchildren and one great-grandchild. Her favorite pastimes are reading, painting, and spending time with family.